Volunteers
and
volunteering

NIACE lifelines in adult learning

The *NIACE lifelines in adult learning* series provides straightforward background and information, accessible know-how and useful examples of good practice for all practitioners involved in adult and community learning. Focusing in turn on different areas of adult learning these guides are an essential part of every practitioner's toolkit.

Volunteers and volunteering

Janet Swinney

Published by the National Institute of
Adult Continuing Education (England and Wales)

21 De Montfort Street
Leicester LE1 7GE
Company registration no. 2603322
Charity registration no. 1002775

First published 2005

The *NIACE lifelines in adult learning series* is supported by the Adult
and Community Learning Fund. ACLF is funded by the Department
for Education and Skills and managed in partnership by NIACE and
the Basic Skills Agency to develop widening participation in adult learning.

promoting adult learning

NIACE has a broad remit to promote lifelong learning
opportunities for adults. NIACE works to develop
increased participation in education and training,
particularly for those who do not have easy access
because of barriers of class, gender, age, race,
language and culture, learning difficulties and
disabilities, or insufficient financial resources.

www.niace.org.uk

Cataloguing in Publication Data
A CIP record of this title is available from the British Library

Designed and typeset by Boldface
Printed in Great Britain by Russell Press, Nottingham

ISBN 1 86201 187 7

Acknowledgements

Huge thanks are due to all those groups and individuals who contributed to the development of this work. We met many remarkable people in the course of gathering the material contained within these pages. It was a privilege to be entrusted with the personal accounts and insights people shared with us. We wish everyone well with their endeavours and hope that their aspirations will be fulfilled.

Janet Swinney
Writer

Kay Snowdon
Research assistant

Contents

Note to the reader

Inspirations: refer to case studies and examples of interesting practice.
Glossary: the meanings of the words underlined in the text can be found in the glossary on page 47

Paul in the grounds at Bensham Grove

Introduction

Organisations built partly or wholly on the unpaid effort of volunteers are many and various, and have been a longstanding feature of life in the United Kingdom. They range from the very small and entirely informal to the very large and highly structured. They include small community organisations and self-help groups with no paid staff, voluntary organisations with one or more paid employees, large charitable organisations dedicated to a specific cause and local authority services with a focus on community development or adult learning.

This book looks at the experiences of people who took the step into volunteering, sometimes to help others learn, and sometimes for entirely other reasons, but who then found themselves on their own journey of learning, discovery and transformation. It examines the factors that make volunteering a productive experience, firstly for the volunteer, and secondly for those they work with. And it suggests points that organisations and providers might wish to consider before starting work with volunteers or in order to refine and develop their existing practice. These suggestions take account of the ever-present need to demonstrate performance.

Several of the organisations that contributed insights, case studies and valuable time to the development of this work received finance from the Adult and Community Learning Fund (ACLF) of the Department for Education and Skills, to develop specific projects which involved working with volunteers. This fund was managed jointly by the National Institute of Adult Continuing Education (NIACE) and the Basic Skills Agency (BSA) in the period 1998–2004.

Organisations receiving funding from the ACLF were:

- Norfolk Adult Education Service for their *Living Memory* project;
- Riverside Credit Union, Liverpool;
- Manchester Women's Electronic Village Hall for an internet project for women refugees and asylum seekers where learners also acted as mentors;
- Horizon Housing, East Sussex, for its *Women in Action* mentoring project for women seeking to enter employment;
- Southampton and New Forest MIND, for its drop-in and activities programme run at Marcella House Resource Centre for people dealing with mental health difficulties.

Other organisations and providers were asked to contribute because of their proven expertise in working with volunteers. TimeBank is a national volunteering charity committed to 'connecting and inspiring people to give time and share experiences'. TimeBank was conceived by the founders of Comic Relief and is supported by the Active Communities Unit. Since it was launched in 2000, it has attracted over 60,000 recruits. 'Learning Links' is a not-for-profit organisation working in Hampshire, Portsmouth and the Isle of Wight. It has trained over 550 local residents to act as 'learning champions' in their communities. Art and Soul is based in Portsmouth. It is a small, not-for profit, community arts organisation that depends on volunteers to help run the organisation and stage many of its events. Community Learning Gateshead is a local authority service built on the values and principles of community development. And Northern College for Residential Adult Education near Barnsley in South Yorkshire has a long-standing commitment to enabling working-class people to acquire the knowledge, skills and understanding necessary to be effective community activists and organisers.

Photograph courtesy of The Living Memory Project

1 Policy context

The Chancellor of the Exchequer, the Right Honourable Gordon Brown, MP, declared 2005 to be the Year of the Volunteer. What a landmark for volunteers and volunteering!

It was 1987 when, in the course of an interview with *Woman's Own* magazine, Margaret Thatcher made the memorable statement 'There is no such thing as society'. In all fairness, she did then go on to say, 'It's our duty to look after ourselves and then to look after our neighbour'.

Neighbourliness might be defined as those things we do voluntarily to help out those around us when they're in a tight spot. Add an element of structure – whereby people give their time on a regular basis to do something specific for others they are aware of but may not know on a personal basis, and we have 'volunteering' and 'voluntarism'. Voluntarism helps build social infrastructure, by helping communities, however defined, develop shared understandings, shared knowledge and skills, a sense of mutual obligation and an ever-widening network of contacts.

For many years, central government via local government has provided funding to support the infrastructure that makes voluntarism possible. Ironically, during the years that the Conservatives were in office, at the very time when many hard-pressed communities began to unravel, the voluntary and community sector experienced massive cuts in their funding. The same thing happened to local government services with a weak statutory framework; that is services such as adult and community education, were the ones most likely to be working with volunteers.

When New Labour came to power it inherited a situation where poorer communities were in crisis, caught in a spiral of decline. Many families were without work. Where there was no work, there was no spending money. Where there was no spending money, banks and shops saw no point in maintaining a presence. With no earning power, people's morale and self-esteem were low: anti-social behaviour and inter-racial tensions increased. In short, the whole social and economic infrastructure of some communities was collapsing. Perhaps the first document to recognise the full extent of these issues and to set out some proposals for dealing with them was *Social Justice: Strategies for National Renewal*, the report of the Commission on Social Justice, published in 1994 and commissioned by the Right Honourable John Smith QC, MP.

The government embarked on developing a neighbourhood renewal strategy. Its Social Exclusion Unit established 18 policy action teams. One of these, Policy

Action Team 9, looking at community self-help, was asked to consider how to increase the amount of volunteering and community activity in poor neighbourhoods; how to increase the viability of community groups, and how to encourage the growth of informal mutual support. This team identified a number of barriers to community self-help including:

* lack of energy due to residents' personal circumstances;
* lack of confidence among residents due to low levels of literacy and education, unemployment and a lack of experience of community involvement, committee work and management;
* lack of trust of neighbours resulting from a mobile community, the presence of known criminals in the community and the adverse effects of local housing policies;
* lack of resources and support for emerging community activities;
* the costs of volunteering and community self-help activity – travel, childcare and so on.

Its report also raised issues about the inadequacies of the infrastructure supporting voluntary and community organisations, commenting on the poor resourcing of Councils for Voluntary Service (CVSs) which provide training and advice for their local voluntary and community groups, and the variable performance of local authorities in supporting the voluntary and community sector. It went on to make 33 recommendations about how the situation might be improved. Many of these recommendations have been acted upon.

In 1998, the government's Active Community Unit established a national 'compact' between central government and the voluntary and community sector, setting out a framework for partnership working. Councils in England were required to have local compacts in place by April 2004. The overall aim is to ensure that the voluntary and community sector have a greater voice in shaping local services and in contributing to their delivery. In 2001, the Community Empowerment Fund was introduced. The fund was intended to help increase community involvement by enabling communities to identify key issues and appropriate local solutions. As such, it could be used for training volunteers in relevant skills such as community intervention and the management of groups.

Recognition of the role of volunteers in rebuilding communities and enhancing community capacity in the form of knowledge and skills has steadily grown. This was highlighted in the *Cross-cutting Review of the Voluntary and Community Sector* carried out by HM Treasury in 2002.

In 2004, the government's Civil Renewal Unit published *Firm Foundations*, the report of its review of the support available for community capacity building. Among other things, this document affirmed the importance of a *community development* approach as a means of bringing about long-term change in poorer communities. It also emphasised the importance of learning, and recognised that "Learning should start from people's immediate needs and life experience and should recognise that 'peer learning', or learning through shared experience is often the most effective method". This suggests that there is much scope for volunteers to work as coaches and mentors within their own communities. *Firm Foundations* also draws attention to the need to recognise the importance of communities based allegiances other than geography. These include communities where people's sense of belonging is based on a particular set of circumstances, faith or ethnicity. In this book we will see some examples of how volunteers contribute to groups brought together by shared experience.

While the neighbourhood renewal agenda was unfolding, largely under the auspices of the Office of the Deputy Prime Minister, but also with the involvement of the Home Office, there were developments taking place elsewhere in government in relation to learning and skills. These developments had a bearing on adult and community learning – that is, informal adult learning programmes delivered by local education authorities, further education colleges and the voluntary and community sector.

The Learning and Skills Act 2000, and the subsequent skills strategy, *21st Cen- -tury Skills*, published in 2003, focus largely on the UK's performance in a global economy. The emphasis is on remedying skills shortages and the need to raise educational achievement overall. One of the main areas of concern is the poor levels of basic skills among adults. 2001 saw the launch of the government's *Skills for Life* strategy, intended to:

- improve the literacy and numeracy skills of 1.5 million people by 2005;
- ensure that England has 'one of the best adult literacy and numeracy rates' in the world; and,
- ultimately, eliminate the problem altogether.

The very fact that people with poor levels of literacy and numeracy tend to be living in less well-off communities has meant that providers have expended much effort on engaging with in these communities and involving residents in learning activities that offer palatable ways of improving literacy, language and numeracy skills.

Two additional sources of funding have been particularly helpful in this respect. One was the Adult and Community Learning Fund managed jointly by the National Institute of Adult Continuing Education (NIACE) and the Basic Skills Agency (BSA) between 1998 and 2004. The other was the Link-up Project, funded by the Adult Basic Skills Strategy Unit (ABSSU) of the Department for Education and Skills (DfES) and the Active Community Unit of the Home Office. This project was managed by the Basic Skills Agency (BSA) in partnership with the voluntary sector and other educational providers. Its aim was to 'promote literacy, language and numeracy volunteering'.

More recently, in May 2004, in *A Strategy for the Voluntary and Community Sector and the Learning and Skills Council*, the LSC set out plans for working more effectively with the voluntary and community sector at both national and local levels. It states: 'The interdependence between the sector and the LSC in pursuit of shared aims for learning and skills means the LSC has a strong interest in developing the capacity of sector staff, including volunteers. Workforce development planning at national, regional and local levels should reflect their training needs, and recognise training for unpaid staff as eligible for workforce development funding'.

For providers whose work is community-focused, it can often be difficult to see how the policies and funding streams that emanate from one government department square with those that emanate from another. But the fact is, that as far as policy-makers are concerned, the standing of volunteers and the value of their contribution in furthering <u>sustainable development</u> has never been higher. Now is the time for providers to review their current practice and to take full advantage of the opportunities available to encourage a culture of voluntarism.

Photograph courtesy of The Living Memory Project

2 Why organisations use volunteers

Organisations fall into a number of broad categories in terms of their involvement with volunteers.

Some have the delivery of a particular service to a specific client group as their primary purpose. But the service is enhanced by having additional support from volunteers. In Norfolk, for example, the Adult Education Service was keen to widen participation in lifelong learning to include older people and their carers. Its Living Memory project achieved this in a number of ways: it trained over three hundred carers to deliver a range of learning activities where they worked, and it recruited volunteers and paid tutors to undertake reminiscence work in care homes and community venues. The primary purpose of the *Women in Action* programme run by Horizon Housing is to help women make the transition from home to employment or vocational training. At this point in their lives, women's self-confidence tends to be very low, and the project manager recognised that support in the form of a volunteer mentor who had already been through a similar experience was likely to be very helpful: in other words, she saw that volunteer support was likely to 'add value' to the project. A number of providers, local authorities in particular, use volunteers to assist in the delivery of their *Skills for Life* provision. They recognise the need to give learners a lot of individual attention, but don't have the financial means to employ a paid tutor for every person. Here, volunteers usually assist a paid tutor, providing a level of personal support for the learner which would otherwise be impossible. In all of these situations, volunteers are acting as 'para-professionals' and are expected to train to acquire some sort of specialist knowledge and/or skills to help them carry out their role.

TimeBank is representative of another type of organisation where encouraging volunteering for its own sake is the primary purpose. TimeBank provides a brokerage service, matching volunteers with others who could benefit from knowledge, skills or experience that the volunteer already has. The organisation also runs campaigns to recruit volunteers with specific areas of interest, for example, sport, the arts, the environment and work with refugees. 'TimeBank', says the publicity, 'appeals to people...who know that their time and skills are in demand, but just don't know what to do about it or where to start.' The underlying assumption is that some people have had the opportunity, through education, personal circumstances and general good fortune to develop knowledge, skills, interests and pastimes which are worth sharing with others who have been less fortunate. University settlements,

> "We would not run without volunteers. The whole ethos of credit unions is that they are run by volunteers and we only have paid staff here due to our growth. If the job was taken away from volunteers, then I think ownership and respect from the community would go. Volunteers have got to come from the local community you are serving."
>
> Colin Farrell, Manager, Riverside Credit Union, Speke.

which have a long tradition of 'town and gown' activities, where students carry out voluntary activities within the wider community, also fit within this category.

Some organisations have a dual purpose. Art and Soul Traders is a small not-for-profit company committed to initiating and developing community arts activities in the heart of Portsmouth, one of the city's poorest areas. It runs children's workshops, and adult learning courses in video-making, music production, creative computing and DJing, as well as supporting local artists, running special events and mounting exhibitions. However, the co-ordinators quickly realised that many of the tasks involved in all of this could not be carried out without the aid of volunteers. 'We just never, ever have enough money to do anything,' says Emma, the project co-ordinator. But many of the people who walked in off the street offering help were fragile and in need of support themselves. Soon, developing volunteers became parts of Art and Soul's core business.

Then, there are others who see developing people as their primary purpose. What the volunteers then go on and do is negotiable. Community Learning Gateshead, for example, sees recruiting and 'growing' volunteers as central to its mission to develop social capital and community infrastructure, enabling communities to become self-managing. The service supports community associations in every settlement in the borough. These associations, with the assistance of a community education worker, are responsible for managing the affairs of their community education centre. The service also runs projects where learners are encouraged to take up roles on the management committee, and it seconds salaried staff to voluntary organisations to help them develop their work.

Last, but not least, there are voluntary organisations that come into existence because people perceive a gap in services. June, a graduate of Northern College's neighbourhood animateur course, with no prior experience as a professional worker, established the Barnsley Beacon, a support group for people struggling to cope with the impact of drug abuse on their families. She felt that although abusers themselves receive support, no-one was helping the people around them deal with the devastation inflicted upon them. The Speke estate, Liverpool, one of the most deprived areas in the UK, was bereft of financial services when a group of local people decided to establish Riverside Credit Union. Credit unions are financial co-operatives owned and controlled by their members. They offer savings and loans at rates that are extremely good value. For people on a low income, they offer a way out of poverty. Now that Riverside Credit Union is well-established and has grown in size, it employs two paid staff as managers, to oversee the day-to-day business, but volunteers are still at the heart of the organisation, carrying out most of the decision-making. There are 15 board members, three internal supervisors and three cashiers, all of whom are volunteers from the local community.

So, voluntarism serves different purposes in different contexts. Working with volunteers can improve the quality of service delivery. By sharing knowledge, skills and interests volunteers can help others broaden their horizons. Cultivating voluntary involvement in community activity can lead to the development of communities where people are mutually supportive. And voluntary action can generate services and facilities where none existed. What's more, where volunteers work with others whose experiences they have shared, their organisation often gains credibility with the group they want to reach.

Points to consider

If you're part of an organisation that doesn't employ volunteers:

- Might you be able to carry out your role more effectively with the support of a volunteer work-force?

"Volunteers are the bedrock of our service. We employ them in every kind of situation and role from unstructured to structured. The only factor that they have in common is that they all have to undergo the criminal activities check. A high proportion of our salaried staff started off as volunteers."
Kevin Pearson, Adult Learning Manager, Community Learning Gateshead

"We felt the best way to get people in run-down communities back into learning was for local people to act as advocates themselves. Word spreads quickly that way. And it dispels stereotypes about people from large, monolithic organisations swooping in on unsuspecting communities to do their bit."
Clare Ashley, Community Education and Quality Manager, Learning Links, talking about the PALs Project.

If you're part of an organisation already working with volunteers:

- What is your primary goal?
- Is it the right primary goal?
- Is it time to shift the emphasis?

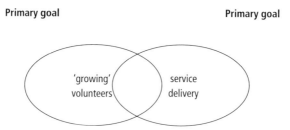

What's more: some organisations are 'growing' learners to become volunteers, while others are 'growing' volunteers to become learners. Some do both. Is there a way that your organisation could embed this cycle into the way it operates?

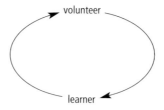

3 Why do volunteers do it? (and what this might mean for you...)

It's often assumed that when people volunteer they have a clear idea of what they want to do, a special skill to offer, a sense of altruism and some time on their hands. This cameo certainly applies in some cases, but probably in a minority. Others find themselves at a crossroads in their lives where, suddenly, they feel they want to make a difference, and they don't very much mind how they make their contribution: it could be digging ditches on an environmental project, or mentoring a young person excluded from school. The desire for change can be triggered by moving through a particular stage in the life-cycle such as getting the children off to school, or retiring or finding oneself in a paid job that is going nowhere. It can also be triggered by an unexpected change in circumstances, or a personal trauma that gives pause for thought. In this kind of situation, the desire for change can be tied up as much with wanting to make a difference to one's own life as with wanting to make a difference to others'. Another common motivation is a sense of alienation: simply having a sense that there must be more to life than being confined within one's own four walls, of wanting to feel connected to the rest of the human race. However these transformations come about, all are underpinned by fellow-feeling, the desire to part of something that is bigger than ourselves.

"Volunteers pour out of the woodwork! We have a special location here in Victoria Park, and a lovely building, and some would tell you it sits on a ley line! In between the affluent quayside and here, there's real poverty, both in terms of culture and resources – homes with no books in them and nothing to draw with – so this is a resource for people. The door is always open. The only rule is you can't come in if you smell of alcohol." Emma Wright, Project Co-ordinator, Art and Soul Traders, Portsmouth

"I had been self-employed for 30 years. In 1999, my mother, who was a retired ward sister, was mugged on the way home from church. She hit her head against a house wall and then again on the pavement and was completely unconscious. For a woman who was so independent, it changed her life in just a few minutes. She was admitted to hospital. I was so, so angry. I was working nights, and couldn't do much to help her. She went through a long time when she needed rehabilitation. She ended up partially sighted – couldn't go out of the flat on her own – and in sheltered accommodation. I was so mad. Then later, in 2000, personal circumstances just made me walk away from everything I'd got. I lost my business. I lost my house. I lost everything. But one thing I was determined to do. It had been such a harrowing time – we'd had so very little time together – and I decided to some take time out. It was just in that time, one day I'd taken my mother out shopping and I saw an advert asking for volunteers for victim support and I launched myself into that. I gave it everything. I visited over 400 people who had been victims of crime ranging from purse-snatching to house-breaking to being threatened with violence. In that time, I was going through my own personal dilemma, wondering: what should I do? where do I go? and wondering about the situation where poor people always seem to come off worst. For more affluent people, crime is more like an inconvenience and they have insurance cover, but for people who have very little and can hardly afford to replace what they lose, it's different. What struck me was the inequality of it all and that's what started me off wanting to work in the community."

Dave – graduate, community animateur course, Northern College, and now community regeneration officer

The fact that volunteers have such varied starting points means that organisations need to think carefully about how to attract them, or how to position themselves so that volunteers can find them when they need to. A service provider looking for people with a specific type of expertise obviously has to advertise for it. But organisations working with volunteers as an end in itself, who expect people to bring only their common humanity, will need to think about the matter differently. The same is true for organisations with a dual purpose (see previous chapter).

"It was about 13 years ago my life started to change. It was round about the time of the Jamie Bulger case. I just could not get over it – I was really shocked. Not just for Jamie Bulger, but for the young people that had committed the crime, because their lives were over as well. I thought: what would happen if my own child did this? I sort of looked back on my own past: how I'd failed in my education, and how some people had been significant in my life and had actually helped me move on and I thought maybe I could do the same for other people. In my naïvety I thought all young people needed was someone to listen to them, and I was lucky I had had that. So off I went to the community centre to be a volunteer."

John – full-time salaried community education worker,

Springwell, Community Learning Gateshead

"My husband was teacher-trained in the early 1970s and did community work as his secondary subject. By the time he had finished his training, they weren't looking for so many teachers but he managed to get a job as a community worker. He was working at the YMCA down at North Shields and was really keen to do a residential and he couldn't get a female member of staff to go with him. So he said, so that his boss wouldn't prevent him from going, 'Well it's OK, my wife will come with us.' So I was dragged, kicking and screaming, to this residential and we had a wonderful, wonderful time. I never really thought about working with people before, but that changed things. I did a lot of voluntary work after that, club nights and going on camping weekends, and taking my own kids with us."

Eleanor – part-time paid worker,

Gateshead Young Women's

Project

"I was unemployed for about eight years after having one nervous breakdown after another. The doctor said, "Don't even think of going back to work of any kind". Being a woman of some intelligence and quite a lot of motivation at times, that was so frustrating. It was like being told I was worthless. It had a really bad effect. Towards the end of the eight years I did start to do some voluntary work for the Salvation Army day centre for the elderly. The manager there sent me on a two-day course in reminiscence work run by the Living Memory project. And I fell in love straight away, really because I felt a sense of purpose which was just what I was looking for."

Sarah, volunteer reminiscence worker, Living Memory

Project, Norfolk Adult Education Service

Points to consider

- **Publicity strategy**
- Does your strategy for 'putting yourself about' match your organisation's goals?
  - Does the content of your publicity material (in whatever medium) reflect an awareness of the factors that might make members of the public want to get involved in your work? That is, does it say how volunteers might benefit, and not just what your organisation is looking for?
  - Does your material appear in places where people thinking about a change in their lives might see (or hear) it?
  - Do you make use of media that the people you're trying to reach are likely to be receptive to?
- **Profile** – does your organisation have a high profile among the community it aims to serve? Is it known as a place where volunteers are welcomed?
- **Networks** – is your organisation well-known to other community organisations with which it might have common cause? Are working relationships mutually rewarding and productive? Can you use them to reach potential volunteers?
- **Capacity** – Do volunteers receive a warm welcome, when they first make contact with your establishment?
- **Supply and demand** – Are all comers welcome at any time of the year, or do you need to think about supply and demand? In other words, how can you avoid over-recruiting and keeping volunteers waiting a long time before they start work with you?

"You need to know your community. We have a lot of knowledge because we have grown up here. You need to be able to spot key activists or members of the community. We have never had to advertise to recruit – it's word of mouth. People who have been involved talk to their friends... they just need the encouragement to come forward. People just come as we have such a standing in the community. People know what goes on here: they like what we do."
Emma Wright, Project Co-ordinator, Art and Soul Traders, Portsmouth

"The reason I volunteered? One: I had some time to do it, and two: I'd been interested for about or year or so. When I heard about TimeBank, it seemed an opportunity to get started, as opposed to just thinking about it. I only had a brief explanation of what they did with refugees, but it seemed like something I wanted to get involved with. I went to a training day – very straightforward – and it all seemed a lot easier than I imagined. They put me with a mentor almost immediately. I feel I'm being helpful and I want to give something back to people who need a bit of help here and there. I work for a local government quango, and I've got quite a comfortable job – I feel a bit cosseted really. This gives me a different perspective, to see everyday problems that you don't even recognise as problems, but for people starting life afresh without having a choice in the matter, they are."

Refugee mentor and teacher of English, Time Together project, TimeBank

Manchester Women's Electronic Village Hall (MWEVH) focuses on how information technology impacts on women's lives, and on equipping women to cope with it on their own terms. The purpose of their mentoring project was to reach and work with women who were refugees and asylum seekers, developing their access to useful IT resources, and developing their skills in the use of IT. The project steering group was determined to reach women from a wide range of ethnic minority communities to be mentors as well as learners. Using existing networks was the key. The first nine months of the project were spent networking among refugee support organisations as well as refugee communities. MWEVH became a member of the Greater Manchester Refugee (GMR) Smartgroup, an e-mail newsgroup with over 200 subscribers. This became an essential tool for recruitment. In some cases, mentors were able to make recommendations (about potential learners) as a direct result of their involvement within existing community groups. Networking by various means meant the MWEVH was able to demonstrate a commitment to the client group while keeping informed of legislative changes and gaining knowledge about different communities and faith groups. In turn, this informed the project team's work. They were able to show cultural sensitivity and an awareness of the difficulties faced by individuals – based on the final project report.

4 The early stages

Naturally, anyone who volunteers their services wants to feel that they haven't done so in vain: they want to feel welcomed, valued, supported, reassured and given some direction about how to carry out their role. However, once the 'hellos' are over, organisations vary enormously in terms of how they set about this task. As in other matters, this depends largely on how they see themselves and their primary role. Basically, the closer an organisation is to employing volunteers as para-professionals, the more formal its systems and procedures are likely to be: the more emphasis it places on the development of the volunteers as an end in itself, the less formal its approach.

Selection – or finding a role that fits

Having said this, few organisations operate selection procedures that are so formal that they resemble job interviews, even if they are looking for people with specific skills and expertise. Some offer open days or evenings where members of the public can find out more about what volunteering is likely to involve and then opt out if they decide it's not for them. Smaller organisations often manage to find the time to talk to potential volunteers on a one-to-one basis about what sort of help they would welcome, and how the volunteer might be able to contribute. Some even tailor roles to suit particular people. 'Growing' volunteers can be an open-ended process of dialogue and negotiation extending over a number of years. Managing the 'evolution' of unconfident volunteers into skilled and trained employees can be an important part of a Community Education worker's role, for example. Few organisations ever flatly reject people who have volunteered. What they may do, if they can't find a suitable niche for them, is signpost them elsewhere.

Job descriptions and agreements

How necessary is it to define exactly what a volunteer gets up to, and how often or how long they do it for? This, again, depends on the type of organisation. Providers who employ volunteers as para-professionals, for example, as learning assistants or as learning mentors, tend to make more use of job descriptions than others, and to be more specific about the commitment they are looking for.

In *Skills for Life* provision, for example, job descriptions can be used to delineate how the roles of paid and unpaid tutors complement one another and help

"We are into equal opportunities and our ethos is that everybody has something to give. So it's not for us to say who hasn't got the skills. It's about identifying what particular skills they have. So they would come in, we would have a little talk with them, show them the various aspects of what is done here, letting them have a go at each one, and they find out what they are good at, or they say, 'I like the sound of that. I'll stick at that. For example, one woman said she didn't want to go on [our training course], and would make the tea and tidy up. But we encouraged her and now she's on the Board of Directors."
Colin Farrell, Manager, Riverside Credit Union

avoid misunderstandings about who is responsible for what. Job descriptions can also be important where volunteers work in situations where learners may present sensitive personal and emotional issues. In these circumstances, job descriptions can be a useful means of safeguarding the volunteer by placing parameters on their role, and indicating the sort of situation where they need to ask for professional help. In other kinds of organisation, job descriptions are thought to be unnecessary, if not downright off-putting. Some organisations have arrived at a half-way position where they avoid job descriptions, but use written agreements setting out the rights and responsibilities not just of the volunteer, but of the

"All the time you're on the look out for that spark people have and you try and get them to develop that. I wouldn't force people into things. I don't want to set them up to be a failure... because I know what that's like."
John – full-time salaried community education worker, Springwell, Community Learning Gateshead

"Finding out what people really want is the key. That's my first aim. I have a huge database in my head of contacts and other organisations that need volunteers. People never feel rejected if you say, 'I'm really looking to find out what it is you really want to do.' If they don't know what they want, I say 'Get in touch once you have thought about all these ideas and contacts I have given you.'"
Mentoring project manager, Manchester Women's Electronic Village Hall

"First we have a chat. I explain what we do and the things we have coming up. Then we have a form for the volunteer to fill in. This asks for basic information: what special skills or interests they'd like to share, what things they'd like to do, even if they've got no experience, and then we find areas they can work in. I think our volunteer programme is special because it is so broad, so open, so welcoming, and people don't have to have anything in mind when they walk through the door."
Emma Wright, Project Co-ordinator, Art and Soul Traders, Portsmouth

organisation itself. The Women in Action project, run by Horizon Housing, takes this a step further by asking mentors to set up their own ground-rules with learners.

Time commitment

As far as time commitment is concerned, organisations working with volunteers as para-professionals tend to ask for a regular commitment over a number of months or years. Those that see the development of volunteers as their primary role have a more open-ended approach. Ironically, this does not seem to affect the length of time volunteers stay, only their pattern of attendance. Where volunteers feel that they are always welcome, they may continue to contribute over many years, though their contribution might be intermittent. There are volunteers who work for as little as two hours per week and others who are doing what is almost a full-time job. There are no hard-and-fast rules about this. Only the organisation and the volunteer can decide what suits them.

Induction

There is no one way to go about induction either. Some organisations combine self-selection with initial training, organising events where the volunteer and the organisation can find out about each other. Some follow an initial meeting between volunteer and staff member with more extended training that prepares them for their role. It's at this point that some organisations choose to introduce

"'Way Out in Gateshead is the outdoor education unit of Community Learning Gateshead, offering a wide range of programmes from short two-hour tasters to five-day residentials to groups from across the service, including people with disabilities and older learners. Volunteers play an important part in its work, helping to organise and deliver the programmes. We have quite a formal selection process, actually. We have an open evening where a member of staff gives a presentation followed by questions and answers. Then there's an application form for people to complete, with a closing date, because we take people on in batches. But what we make clear throughout is that what we're interested in is your attitude and willingness to make a contribution. We don't care how high, how fast or how deep you can do things: we're not interested in your death-defying tales of machismo. It's your motivation and people skills that are really important."
Bill Haylock, Senior Development Worker, Way Out In Gateshead, Community Learning Gateshead

"The Women in Action mentoring project is one component of a wider Women in Action programme that provides pre-vocational training and practical support for women who wish to start or return to work or further education in East Sussex. Participants in the programme are offered assistance with work placements and further training. Through mentoring, participants are supported in their transition from training into their work placement.

Mentors receive a job description that sets out their purposes, tasks and activities and the personal attributes necessary to be an effective mentor. The mentor and mentee then go on to draw up their own agreement that contains the essential components of the mentoring relationship including where meetings will take place, the time, confidentiality agreements, the objectives and duration of the mentoring process as well as practical arrangements around travel and childcare. The agreement also sets out the protocol for cancellation of meetings."

Based on the project's interim evaluation report

"TimeBank's Time Together programme, instigated by David Blunkett, MP, aims to provide mentors for refugees to help them find their feet in British society. The programme is established in London, Birmingham and Glasgow, and attracts large numbers of volunteers. At any one time there are about 130 mentor/mentee pairs working in London and 50 pairs working in Birmingham and Glasgow.

Time Together runs a one-day training course for new volunteers. This covers a lot of ground. Former mentors and mentees are invited to come along to talk about their experiences, and we show a documentary about the project. Refugees who have not yet been matched with mentors also attend. They spend some time in a group on their own where they are briefed about what to expect from the scheme. Then mentors and refugees have the chance to meet and to learn about the roles and responsibilities of each party. The whole approach is very practical. They do some structured exercises together. There's lots of talking around refugee issues and the practical solutions to them. We provide a handbook for the mentors that provides guidance on how to carry out the role and the issues involved. At the end of this experience, the refugees and the mentors are matched. What we've heard during discussions is very helpful in this respect."

Sarah Arnold, Project Manager, Time Together

SPIRATIONS

"Learning Links requires potential learning advocates (PALs) to under-take a course spread over ten weeks. This is delivered in partnership with local colleges of further education, but always covers the same ground, that is: the background to the project, why we need it, what it means to be a learning champion and the sort of things you can expect to be a part of once you are one.

The induction pack includes the written agreement that governs the relationship we have with volunteers. For example, Learning Links undertakes to support volunteers in their role and further development, to reimburse costs incurred in carrying out the role, to make sure that volunteers are treated fairly and that they have some recourse if they run into difficulties. At the same time, we expect volunteers to attend monthly support meetings with their area co-ordinator, and to follow a certain code of conduct when they're dealing with other people. For instance, it would be disastrous in local communities if volunteers infringed roles of confidentiality, or didn't treat other people with respect. We also expect volunteers to relay what they find out about local learning needs, as the main point of the exercise is to help us to respond to these. The third part of the pack covers things like how to keep yourself safe and provides suggestions on how to raise the profile of learning in local communities. This includes things like taking part in parents' evenings, talking to people at the school gate and accompany-ing someone who is nervous about attending a course for the first time."

**Clare Ashley, Community Education and Quality Manager,
Learning Links**

the written agreement that will underpin the relationship between themselves and the volunteer. This is discussed in some depth during the training programme. Other forms of induction include having the chance to try out the new role under the supervision of a more experienced person. Or simply talking on a one-to-one basis about what the volunteer's role will involve and trying to dispel any misgivings and misunderstandings the volunteer might have. Generally speaking, where organisations recruit large numbers of volunteers, or where they expect them all to carry out broadly similar roles, they are more likely to develop a tightly structured induction programme.

"'Introduction to Mentoring' course. A pilot course based on 'bought-in' materials was delivered in 2001, but the materials had been devised for a mentoring programme for young people and were inappropriate for women returners. Money from the ACLF enabled staff to develop and customised training materials and a training workbook suitable for the mentoring of women returners.

The following are covered through the mentoring training programme: what mentoring is, the mentoring process, counselling and coaching, valuing diversity, verbal and non-verbal communication, listening skills, understanding motivation, effective questioning techniques, learning styles and relationship skills.

The formal training element takes place over 26 weeks and includes 108 hours of tutor contact time, with a minimum of 78 hours of independent study. Participants attend a training workshop delivered one morning a week over ten weeks.

This is now a bespoke training programme accredited at Level 2. The qualification already existed, but has been refocused by Women in Action."

Based on the project's interim evaluation report

Riverside Credit Union runs a three-day induction course for its volunteers. This covers the history of credit unions and the philosophy behind them. It looks at the communication skills required of volunteers, explores some of the mathematical knowledge and skills needed by people working in a Credit Union and introduces the paperwork volunteers will need to be familiar with to be able to handle financial transactions. The supporting handbook for volunteers was produced with the help of the ACLF. Additional sessions on computer literacy and basic skills are available according to need.

Colin Farrell, Manager, says, 'People start volunteering first, and then do the course. In that way some skills emerge and others are identified that need developing. We believe in learning by doing and sharing skills. We rely on people to support each other, which they do. They also have a mentor. We don't put volunteers down: we create an atmosphere where they feel they can ask any questions without embarrassment.'

"Eighteen volunteers were recruited for the Living Memory project. We had a long and intensive induction process and there were various points along the way at which people could drop out if they felt it wasn't for them. First of all, I had an in-depth chat with enquirers on the phone about the role of the volunteer. Then I sent them an information pack. Then they had a face-to-face interview with me. Then we offered a training course on reminiscence work. And then, of course, we explained that we required a sustained time commitment, so this might have been a deterrent for some. Then there was the opportunity to shadow an existing volunteer or tutor. Those who were still with us at this point continued for about two and a half years unless, of course, they moved into paid employment or were spurred on to higher education."
Margaret Plummer, Project Manager, Living Memory Project, Norfolk Adult Education Service

Points to consider

- Is it time to revisit the way volunteers join your organisation? Have you got induction practices that are fit-for-purpose?
- Are there certain skill sets and attitudes you definitely need volunteers to bring, or do you think it's preferable to work with whatever people have to offer?
- How tightly does the role of the volunteer need to be defined in your organisation? Would job descriptions or written agreements be helpful in defining roles?
- What sort of time commitment and pattern of attendance do you think would be appropriate for volunteers to give to your organisation? Are you going to accept whatever the volunteer offers? Or will you suggest a commitment, or even stipulate one?
- Do volunteers need the opportunity to hear more about what your organisation does before deciding whether or not to make a commitment?

- What's the best way to ease volunteers into your organisation? Do you have time to talk to them on an individual basis, or do you need to organise some sort of induction event?
- Is there stuff volunteers **must** know before they start work with you? If so, what's the best way to convey this?
- Could existing volunteers and service users play a part in describing the work of your organisation to newcomers?
- Would providing volunteers with mentors be desirable/feasible/affordable?

'Pushing the Possibilities' programme

Photo courtesy of Way Out In Gateshead

5 Ongoing training, development and support

This chapter is about things organisations can do to remove the obstacles to people volunteering, to help keep them on board once they have taken the first step and to help them make the most of the assets they bring. Support for volunteers can take a variety of forms ranging from the practical to the personal.

Practical support

As the government's policy action team on community self-help noted, people can be deterred by the costs involved in volunteering. Providing childcare and travel costs helps overcome this barrier. Many providers offer this kind of support while volunteers are carrying out their induction training, but some also reimburse the costs they incur while carrying out their volunteering duties. Practical support can also be an important means of indicating to volunteers that their services are valued and some organisations have thought of imaginative ways of providing it.

> "We try to provide volunteers with lots of incentives. We run a voucher scheme. Basically, volunteers receive stamps for the work they do, and we've worked out a rate for the different types of things they might be involved in. So, for example, assisting at a publicity event for 2-4 hours earns 25 stamps, while introducing a friend who completes the Accessing Lifelong Learning course and becomes a learning champion themselves earns 50 stamps. At the end of each month, the stamps can be exchanged for vouchers and used in shops like Tesco, Asda or M&S. It's not a huge amounts of money, but it helps. And we've made sure the scheme isn't at odds with the benefits system."
>
> **Clare Ashley, Community Education and Quality Manager, Learning Links**

"You have to give volunteers a good experience – to make them feel valued. We have regular get-togethers to discuss our work. I always try and choose a very nice venue with very good food, and include some activity that will be pleasurable, like aromatherapy. So you're giving the volunteers something in return."
Margaret Plummer, Project Manager, the Living Memory Project, Norfolk Adult Education Service.

"All of our materials for the PALs project is translated into Bengali and Cantonese. Braille and audio translations are also available. In fact, any materials can be made available in any format. And we can provide learning support assistants."
Clare Ashley, Community Education and Quality Manager, Learning Links

"Initially, some women had problems finding our centre because it's not in the centre of town, and failed to turn up for appointments. This included two women coming on public transport and one in a car. The project worker addressed this problem by ordering taxis on account. There were several advantages [to this arrangement]: it reduced all the initial hurdles about actually finding the centre, as well as concerns about self-confidence, language skills and computer knowledge. It also made it much easier for the project worker to plan, as there was a greater likelihood of the women turning up. Once women were confident about the location of the centre, they were encouraged to travel by public transport."
Manchester Women's Electronic Village Hall, mentoring project – based on final report

Continuous professional development

Helping volunteers embark on a process of continuous professional development not only benefits the volunteer, but benefits the organisation, and is an important part of achieving the longer-term goal of building social and human capital in communities. There are some ready-made courses for volunteers that lead to nationally recognised qualifications. These include the Level 2 certificate in adult learner support (City and Guilds 9295) which has been used extensively in *Skills for Life* programmes. Volunteers gaining this certificate can then progress to Level 3 courses in Adult Literacy or Adult Numeracy support. Other qualifications available to volunteers, and offered by City and Guilds are National Vocational Qualifications (NVQs) in Community Development Work Levels 2–4 and Youth Work, Levels 2–3. Organisations that support the voluntary and community sector such as Community Service Volunteers also offer short training courses on various aspects of running and managing voluntary organisations, and this type of training is often open to volunteers. Information about organisations supporting the voluntary and community sector is given in Chapter 7.

Some organisations, having developed training programmes to meet their own needs have had them accredited by the Open College Network (OCN). Qualifications listed on the OCN database that are relevant to volunteers include 'Working with Young People' Levels 2 and 3 and the 'NAYCP Training Programme' at Levels 1 – 3 and 'Managing Your Own Voluntary/Community Organisation' at Level 3.

Following the development of its customised 'Introduction to Mentoring' programme at Level 2, the Women in Action project went on to develop a new accredited training programme at Level 3.

"The advanced mentoring programme was developed in response to demand from mentors. It gives credit for the time spent in the practical mentoring of mentees. It was also intended to enable mentors to share their mentoring experiences and provide a supportive environment for active mentors. There are five learning outcomes to do with demonstrating understanding of what is meant by 'mentoring', creating a supportive atmosphere which encourages learning and personal growth in others, facilitating the client's learning and growth through coaching, giving support and advice to others and monitoring and reviewing the progress and personal growth of others. Learners are expected to reflect upon and improve their own practice."

Women in Action mentoring project – based on the interim evaluation report

A good example of organisation developing, and gaining recognition for, its customised training is Learning Links who has had its Learning Champions course accredited at Level 2 through OCN. Then there's the induction programme for volunteers run by Riverside Credit Union Although it doesn't lead to a Level 2 qualification in its own right, it can be used to contribute to a Level 2 qualification achieved elsewhere. Some providers have managed to develop or establish fully-fledged progression routes for volunteers that open the door to paid employment. These have been designed to meet particular local needs but could be applicable elsewhere.

Northern College's neighbourhood animateurs project is aimed at people from a wide variety of backgrounds and educational experience who wish to embark on community work, or who are already engaged in it, but wish to develop their knowledge and skills. The training programme is structured around a number of week-long residential courses, although students can take up other training opportunities available within the college, and also to carry out a research exercise based on their own community. The key elements of the course are: What is Community Development?; Economic and Political Context; Project Cycle Management; and Communication Skills for Community Activists. Students' work can be accredited at any level between 1 and 3. The parameters of the course are: at one end students can simply undertake unaccredited training or, at the other, they can complete a 16-credit Level 3 award, leading into employment or a higher education course such as the Community Regeneration degree course run by Northern College in partnership with Sheffield Hallam University.

Based on the project evaluation report

In Gateshead, volunteers are gently nudged on to the service's part-time introduction to community education (ICE) course. This lasts for 21 sessions, includes a residential weekend and places a large emphasis on understanding power structures and countering oppressive practices in society. Following this, volunteers are eligible to become part-time paid community education workers. From there they follow a nationally recognised route, progressing on to a part-time workers' course and then to degree level courses. At this point, they become eligible for full-time employment.

'A high value is placed on the contribution that volunteers make to the process of community capacity building... A clear career route is available to them, with professionally accredited training at each stage of progression... From the 266 learners who have taken accredited community education worker courses over the past 15 years, 186 have taken up part-time paid work in the service and five have become full-time workers. In addition, others are working in other council departments or public sector organisations. Many of those who start as volunteers have few or no previous qualifications.

Adult Learning Inspectorate report, Gateshead Council, 2003

The impact of training and development programmes on participants can be dramatic:

'Walking across that road to come up here was terrifying because I didn't know what to expect. I thought they would be all intellectual types and how would I get on? But I'm now much more confident. It was supportive. All students supported you and not just the staff. There was always someone with you who could help you.'

'We had people from all different backgrounds, and we all worked together – Iain learned me about computers for example – and you realised you had something to offer as well. The tutors managed to get the best out of everybody.'

'I grasped at every opportunity there was – visiting a social enterprise in Liverpool, for example.'

'It took me places I'd never thought of – for example going off to do a community audit, and then going on to train volunteers to do their own.'

June, Freda, Dave and Iain talking about their experiences as students on Northern College's neighbourhood animateurs programme.

'I did the ICE course which I really enjoyed. It opened up my mind to things I had never ever thought about like disability – like how to arrange a night out that was accessible for everybody – and we did have people who were disabled on the course. That started things moving. I started reflecting on my own life. My attitudes started to change. I saw I'd got all these sexist, racist attitudes without even knowing it. Then I went on to do the part-time youth work course that made me want to do even more. And I thought, I wonder if I could do this full-time? And I thought I probably had no chance of getting into university for a degree course with one GCSE and a part-time youth work qualification but I did go for the interview, and I had a terrible interview, but I got a place – I couldn't believe it – and three years later I had a degree and I got a job before I finished my degree.'

John, full-time salaried community education worker, Springwell, Community Learning Gateshead.

Personal support

But perhaps what volunteers appreciate most of all is personal support, and there seems to be no length that some individuals and organisations won't go to support their volunteers.

After eight years of unemployment due to mental health difficulties, Sarah started work with the Living Memory project as a volunteer reminiscence worker.

'I'd come to think of myself as someone who was totally unreliable and who couldn't take the strain of any organised activity, and by being a volunteer I found that I could do things. Through spending several months or a year doing voluntary work, I built up the confidence where I did actually turn up. And the really good thing about Margaret [the project manager] was that every time I was ill, I'd end up in hospital and I'd write her a letter and say "I resign. I can't do this for you any more. Just forget me." And every single time she'd ring me up and say, "Thank you for your letter. Let's talk about it when you're feeling better." This meant by the time I was feeling better I was able to say, "I'll do a bit for you still." And that was exactly what I needed. No-one else had ever been so flexible with me. They could cope with the fact that not only was I mentally ill, I was repeatedly and on-goingly mentally ill. Gradually my health got better partly because I had something regular to do. I could do five weeks, have a few weeks off and then do another five weeks of just two hours a week. That sounds minimal, but actually it was a massive amount for someone who had spent years lying in bed doing nothing. And it had an incredible impact on my life: feeling that I was something other than a mental patient. I was someone. I was a reminiscence worker. It gave me an identity and a role'.

Sarah, volunteer reminiscence worker, Living Memory Project, Norfolk Adult Education Service

'What enables volunteers to flourish here? It's all about respect, giving people control and ownership – making them feel a part of what's going. It's very welcoming here and they make people feel comfortable. If you feel comfortable, you behave at your best. Being given power, being trusted to make your own decisions, that's a massive thing. I always remember asking Jo [Project Manager], "Jo, can I do this?" and Jo saying, "Julie, you can do *anything* you want", and that's the general spirit of the place, really.'

Julie, Outreach Support Worker, Young Women's Project, Community Learning Gateshead

ASPIRATIONS

'About 12 years ago I had literacy problems and I had young children, and I was worried about not being able to answer their questions. I eventually plucked up enough courage to ask a retired schoolteacher to help us, which she did. At the same time I went to the local community centre to do voluntary work... The teacher asked me to go to college to do my GCSE and I thought: you've got absolutely no chance of me going to any educational establishment. So I was telling one of my friends who was actually doing the Introduction to Community Education (ICE) course with us, and he said "I'll come with you. I've actually got mine, but I'll do it again." So he went through it all again. So I got my GCSE English. It wasn't a fantastic grade but to me it was HUGE!'

John, full-time salaried community education worker, Springwell, Community Learning Gateshead

'There is supervision on a one-to-one basis once a month – usually for 30 minutes to one hour, but I give the volunteer the option of how much time they want. We sit and talk over issues. However, if any specific issues arise between meetings, I would expect the volunteer to come into my office and offload it – I don't expect them to take it home with them. We can put it in a clear context, and they can go home knowing they have done their job and switch off. If someone wants to move on, I do a wind-down session with them. I talk through the reasons why, and check that they have been happy with the support they have been given. If appropriate, I will help with the transition out. I want to make sure that they feel valued.'

Diane Kitson, Project Manager, Marcella House Resource Centre, Southampton and New Forest MIND

Points to consider

- Is your organisation providing enough appropriate practical support for volunteers so that no-one who wishes to participate as a volunteer is excluded?
- Have you done your best to ensure that there are accredited progression routes for volunteers?
- Are you setting your standards high enough in challenging volunteers to develop themselves?
- Do you provide enough personal support for volunteers?
- Do volunteers in your organisation feel that they and their work is valued? How might you find out, and how might you improve things?

6 Making a difference

How voluntarism changes communities

Many things that enhance the quality of life for communities happen only because volunteers have had a hand in them. Community infrastructure in the form of networks, organisations and activities is steadily built as a result of voluntary activity. People who volunteer develop new relationships with the people they work with and alongside; the benefits of interdependence and mutually supportive action become clear to them and this, in turn, generates a further impetus for community initiatives. Volunteers also increase the asset base that their community can draw upon. Through training, development and experience they grow in knowledge and skills, and these can be reinvested to serve the community.

'Party in the Park was an event that took place in Victoria Park in August. It wasn't about anything but people coming together to have a special day. We had fifty-odd people volunteer to help on the day, and a lot more came to the meetings beforehand to discuss what we were going to do about kids' facilitators, stewards, stage people, raffle-ticket sellers and bric-a-brac stalls. So fifty-odd people gave up an entire day so that 4,000 people could enjoy themselves, and they had the best time doing it. They weren't being done to: it hadn't been organised for them – they were doing it for themselves and for their community. There were people who didn't do very much who enjoyed it so much that they're itching to do it again – can't wait. And there were people who didn't volunteer who watched others enjoying themselves and have asked to be involved next year.'
Emma Wright, Project Co-ordinator, Art and Soul, Portsmouth

'Volunteers are a huge asset to our team. They provide another pair of ears for the people we work with and it just bolsters everything up. A volunteer brings a new pair of hands and new skills. For example, now we have a volunteer driver, we've been able to engage with certain members who haven't got transport and who wouldn't have been able to get here without transport. This is an achievement in itself. Then there's the lady who does computers. A lot of the people we have referred to us have problems getting into social groups, so having someone who can help with that is an asset. She has been able to engage with someone on a one-to-one basis and then help them move into a social group. That has been very useful and has taken pressure off staff so that they can work with other people. The same is true of the poetry class. We can only run that because we have a volunteer who can support the drop-in session.'
Diane Kitson, Project Manager, Marcella House Resource Centre, Southampton and New Forest MIND

'One of the differences volunteers make is that they may be better than the paid staff at some things. Our skiing programmes would hardly be viable without the technical skills of our volunteers. Nor, for example, the sailing trip we did last year down the Caledonian Canal with the Young Women's Project, and this proved to be a profound experience for many of the young women who took part.'
Bill Haylock, Senior Development Worker, Way Out In Gateshead, Community Learning Gateshead

'By the time of the project evaluation, over 450 learners had completed the PALs course, and there had been over 6,000 indirect beneficiaries. In other words, over 6,000 people had been made aware of some of the learning opportunities available in their community. One group of PALs, in Whitchurch went on to establish their own learning group, called the Testbourne Teapot, to overcome social isolation. The Teapot was an immediate success. The group has successfully applied for funding to continue its activities, and to pay for childcare.'
Clare Ashley, Community Education and Quality Manager, Learning Links

'Transport Unlimited is a voluntary organisation providing a reasonably priced transport service to community groups throughout Gateshead. It has several minibuses that can be used for group excursions. Community Learning Gateshead seconds two of us here to act as co-ordinators, but most of our staff are volunteers. We have 240 volunteer drivers on our database, about 12 of whom are called upon each week. Transport can be hired for any time between eight in the morning and eight at night. 608 community groups are registered users of our services, though obviously some use us a lot more than others. Our job is developing volunteers to open doors for other community groups.'
Kevin Surtees, Co-ordinator, Transport Unlimited

'The primary effect of the project was, perhaps, to reduce the women's sense of isolation… The mentors and beneficiaries of mentoring all expressed the importance of e-mail in keeping in touch with family all over the world. Learners who had already used e-mail gained new skills, such as sending and downloading photographic attachments. This was clearly emotionally valued by the women. The project also increased access to news from home…as the mentors learned and passed on information about media resources and methods of finding different language sites on the internet. In terms of local information, participants benefited from web site resources and e-mail [to develop] a much greater awareness of agencies which could help with issues about destitution, legal status, housing, health, jobs, education, schools, etc.'
Manchester Women's Electronic Village Hall, Internet Mentor Project for women refugees and asylum seekers – based on the project's final report

'The thing about here is you'll find paid staff who started off as volunteers still carry on in some voluntary role. So, for example, on a residential project, I might find myself with my boss as a volunteer. People can be chosen to lead sessions on the basis of their qualifications and skills, their gender – if a particular role model is needed – and sometimes their inexperience, to give them the chance to learn. It's got nothing to do with who gets paid.'
Kevin Pearson, Adult Learning Manager, Community Learning Gateshead

How volunteering changes individuals

So much for the impact of voluntarism on communities, what about the impact volunteering has on the volunteers themselves?

What happened to the graduates of Northern College's neighbourhood animateurs course?

Dave flourishes a business card. He now leads Steel Valley Community Partnership's Regeneration Team. The team is responsible for a wide range of activities including an after-school club, a community laundry and a consultancy service for aspiring community groups. It is also in negotiation with a group planning to restore the Don Valley Railway.

Iain is unemployed but spends six days a week helping community groups develop their IT skills and produce their own stationery. He's presently contemplating going to university.

As she came to the end of the course, Freda got a paid job with a regeneration partnership where she was responsible for 18 projects, including a community garden, youth club, walking group and a befriending group. She's since given this up and is looking for a role that is more in line with her political ideals. In the meantime, she works as a volunteer with the Barnsley Beacon.

The Beacon has gone from strength to strength. It now has its own offices, and has broadened the scope of its activity to cover the wider Barnsley area. June now has a salaried post and eight volunteers to assist her. Last year she was nominated for the Heart of Yorkshire Award.

All of the students emphasise how being on the course has helped them build networks that have served them well now that they are back in the community.

The students describe how their self-image has changed as a result of learning:

'When I got ten credits for my community audit, I said to my sister, "You can't call me thick any more", and she said, "But we never thought you were thick anyway!" But I had to find this out for myself.' – June

'I were absolutely gobsmacked when I was told, "You've got enough credits to go to university." I thought "Blimey, I could never have sat an exam in my life. How have I managed this!"' – Iain

John lost his job some years ago when his company moved its plant to another part of the country. He has been a volunteer with Transport Unlimited for eight or nine years He started off as a driver. He now spends most of his time working in the office, but still does some driving. He particularly enjoys working with Gateshead's community of Hasidic Jews. He works with disabled children from the community, driving them to leisure facilities where they can where they can go swimming and horseriding. 'It gives me real joy to think that I am helping to benefit these children', he says. 'and it's something I look forward to'

When Paul was young man, his only expectation was that he'd be going to prison. 'I was a toe-rag,' he says. 'You wouldn't have wanted to know us. I put my family through a lot. But when I turned 18, I looked at ways of being more positive and started community work.' Paul turned up at Bensham Community Centre, Gateshead, where he expressed an interest in gardening. The community centre is in a listed building. Paul set about restoring the garden to its original glory. He is now the co-ordinator of the Heritage Victorian Garden Project, working with a group of students with learning disabilities. Together they research the types of plants required for the garden and how to cultivate them. Paul says his life has changed completely. 'I now have a healthier lifestyle, greater confidence and a more positive attitude towards people.'

'Tahirou says that our sessions are important to him. They are for me as well. In explaining concepts to him, I have been forced to examine my own culture from new perspectives. I have learned about his culture and life in West Africa, a part of the world of which previously I had very little knowledge. Our relationship has helped me appreciate the difficulties faced, and the tremendous courage shown by individuals who seek asylum in this country. As much as I may give to Tahirou, he gives back to me tenfold.'
Suzanne, mentor of Tahirou, Time Together project, TimeBank. Tahirou fled his country due to persecution, having been wrongfully imprisoned for two years.

Susan was very depressed and isolated after the death of her second child when she was contacted by Gateshead Young Women's project, a learning project for teenage mothers. Gradually, she was coaxed into taking on more and more responsibility within the project, for example, by helping to plan a week's activities for visitors from a similar project in Holland. Eventually, she was asked to join the project's management committee. She has completed management committee training and enjoys committee meetings where she feels she is doing something worthwhile by helping the project that helped her. Susan is now off anti-depressants and able to leave the house whenever she wants to. She has gained Literacy and Numeracy qualifications at Level 3 and certificates in food hygiene and first aid. The day she got her first aid certificate, the woman in front of her at the bus stop collapsed and she had to administer treatment. 'I was really scared and crying, but I managed to do it,' she says, 'and the local newspaper did an article about me afterwards.' Susan is currently looking for two people to nominate her to be a representative on the local primary health care trust.

'I decided I wanted to make reminiscence work my life one way or another, and I got on the City and Guilds 7307 tutor training course using reminiscence as my placement, and actually got through that course – I was completely amazed – and then signed up for the 740, degree-level adult education tutor course and I've just passed that as well. Through getting the 7307, I got some other adult education work teaching people with disabilities things like social skills and assertiveness. I've been doing that for a year. And this last summer I was accepted by the Humanities department at university as an English tutor. And all this has sprung from being a volunteer.'
Sarah, volunteer reminiscence worker,
Living Memory Project, Norfolk
Adult Education Service

So, as we can see, the benefits of volunteering to individuals and communities are inextricably linked: one feeds the other. Develop individuals and you develop communities.

7 Management issues

Staffing

It is clear from everything written so far that working with volunteers, whether or not this is the primary goal of your organisation, is a labour-intensive business. Volunteers flourish best where they are welcomed, guided, encouraged, supported and developed in ways that are sensitive and reassuring. Any service manager or management committee dedicated to developing work with volunteers needs to think about how this level of support can be delivered and who will deliver it. Where there are paid employees, then the responsibility for supporting volunteers needs to be clearly allocated and written into the job descriptions of appropriate personnel. And the way that managers allocate workloads needs to reflect the fact that a significant amount of staff time will need to be spent carrying out this support role which is, in fact, about managing people.

Budgets and funding

Staff time is, of course, money, so annual budget plans need to take account of the amount of financial implications of supporting volunteers. Managers and/or management committees also need to take a view about the extent to which they can fund volunteer activity, for example, by paying childcare, travel and subsistence costs. Figures for these, too, should be included in budget plans.

Of necessity, public and voluntary and community sector organisations are having to become increasingly enterprising in the way they seek out funding from central government funding agencies, European funding bodies, trusts and foundations. Carefully counting the 'hidden' costs of volunteering, and making them an explicit line in your budget alerts everybody in your organisation to the fact that you need to be actively looking for funding to support this dimension of your work.

Don't forget to include the management costs involved in being able to demonstrate how effective your organisation is and the costs implied in getting steadily better at what you do. To learn more about this, read on.

Demonstrating impact

The previous chapter is packed with examples of the impact volunteering can have on the lives of individuals and communities. But funding bodies and agencies concerned with inspection and standards, such as the Adult Learning Inspectorate, want more than this. They want to know just how many people gained, and exactly what it was they gained: they want you to **measure** the difference your work has made. This involves counting and analysing. Measuring impact can be a real challenge for organisations concerned with learning and personal development, because some of the things that are easiest to count seem to be the least important, and some of the things that are most important are difficult to describe, let alone count. Often, this is because the important changes that people experience that are likely have a long-term impact on their lives are bound up with changes in feeling, self-perception and vision – the sort of thing that eludes quick quantification.

However, it can be done. Or at least, it's possible to get closer to measuring the impact of volunteering on volunteers and those around them than might seem the case at first glance. First of all, you need some **performance indicators** – but these should be indicators that you genuinely think will provide a useful insight into the benefits of this aspect of your work and how well your organisation is doing. So, for example, you might choose the following to assess how effective you are in attracting and working with volunteers:

- number of people making contact and offering their services;
- proportion of enquirers who start induction training;
- proportion of those who start induction training who complete it;
- number/proportion of volunteers who complete their induction training who start work with the organisation;
- number of volunteers staying with the organisation for more than one year;
- number of volunteers staying with the organisation for more than two years;
- number of hours contributed by volunteers;
- number of successful projects and activities in which volunteers played a significant role.

But then, what about the longer-term impact of volunteering on volunteers? You might wish to add to your list:

- number/proportion of volunteers going on to further training;
- number/proportion of volunteers entering higher education;
- number/proportion of volunteers entering paid employment;
- number/proportion of volunteers moving into other types of voluntary activity;
- number/proportion of your paid work-force who started off as volunteers;
- number/proportion of volunteers going on to establish community groups and activities of their own.

You could also add indicators that reveal something about how volunteers view their own personal development, such as:

- number/proportion of volunteers who feel that volunteering has improved their self-confidence;
- number /proportion of volunteers who feel that volunteering has increased their skills;
- number/proportion of volunteers who feel that volunteering has increased their sense of belonging to a community;
- number/proportion of volunteers who feel that volunteering has improved their employment prospects;
- number/proportion of volunteers who feel that volunteering has raised their aspirations;
- number/proportion of volunteers who feel that volunteering has improved their quality of life.

Choose indicators that are relevant to your organisation. If they're not listed above, have the courage to devise your own. If there are too many, choose the ones that are really central to your work.

Next you need a **research methodology** and some **research tools**. In other words, you need to figure out how you're going to collect this information and how often. You may be able to gather some information from records and analyse it. In other cases, questionnaires, telephone surveys and group discussions may be more appropriate. For example, you could develop the performance indicators about personal development as follows:

'volunteering has improved my self-confidence'

not at all _____ a fair bit _____ a lot

'volunteering has increased my skills'

not at all _____ a fair bit _____ a lot

'volunteering has raised my aspirations'

not at all_____ a fair bit _____ a lot

Don't fall into the trap of thinking that you have to count everything all the time. Plan ahead. Make a point of gathering information at points only when you think it will yield useful results. What's the point of asking the same volunteers every five minutes if their employment prospects have improved? Do it annually, perhaps, or when they're leaving you, when they've had a chance to do some 'growing'. The old analogy about weighing the pig applies. Frequent weighing doesn't increase the pig's weight.

Think about whose job it will be to collect and analyse this information. Another 'hidden' cost that you need to budget for?

All sound too much? Then hire someone. The Women in Action Project, Learning Links and Northern College all benefited from having someone external come and evaluate their work. This provided them with useful information about the immediate benefits of their and its wider or longer-term impact. Hiring an external evaluator who understands the type of work you do and has good research skills can be attractive to small organisations where staff are carrying out several roles at the same time and don't have time to do another one. An outsider can also bring skills and expertise that an organisation lacks as well as an impartial view. No matter how busy you are, make time to work out an assignment brief before you commission the evaluator. You may be able to commission this work from the Learning and Skills Development Agency via your local Learning and Skills Council.

Quality improvement

An obvious benefit of collecting and analysing information against performance indicators is that you begin to get sight of areas where performance might be improved and, if you're the kind of organisation that writes self-assessment reports, to include them in there as matters needing further attention. The new adult learning inspection regime will allow you to focus attention on things that you think are priorities for sorting out. On the other hand, evaluating the impact of volunteering on volunteers and on their communities might reveal that you are doing something exceptionally well that is worth sharing with others.

Small organisations may wish to link the suggestions made above to the work they are doing in relation to PQASSO (the Practical Quality Assurance System for Small Organisations), while for local authorities, the revised Common Inspection Framework will be more appropriate.

Support for voluntary and community sector organisations

Voluntary and community organisations can draw upon their local Council of Voluntary Service for support. This often includes training for volunteers such as management committee training, training in health and safety and in equal opportunities and diversity. In addition to this, all councils in England should now have their local compact with the voluntary and community sector in place. In reality, local authorities still vary in the extent to which they view supporting the voluntary and community sector and, by implication, volunteers and volunteering as an essential part of their role. However, there are some good examples around. Durham County Council provides advice to local community associations on how develop planning applications which will meet external funding requirements. It also helps them prepare funding applications. Gateshead Council offers an annual award to the outstanding volunteer of the year. This gives a powerful message about how highly the council values the contribution of volunteers to improving the wellbeing of its communities.

To a large extent, the value local authorities place on volunteers and volunteering depends on how strong the tradition of community development has been in various parts of the country. Many local authority managers now need to think again about whether they are doing everything possible to help people become volunteers.

Why?

Because they're worth it.

Paul with his students at Bensham Grove

Photograph courtesy of Bensham Grove

8 Check it out

Good practice

Starts with re-examining your organisation's mission and considering whether or not working with and developing volunteers is, could or should be central to what you do, or is, alternatively, a means to helping you achieve a primary purpose.

Next, make sure that your policies, procedures and protocols all reflect whatever your decision is regarding the above. In other words, make sure they are all fit for purpose. For example:

- decide on the best way to let your community know that volunteer help is welcomed;
- make sure that people can find you when they need to, and/or you can find them;
- think about ways of reaching potential volunteers at points in their lives when they are likely to be looking for change and development;
- research and use whatever means of promotion and publicity are available in your community;
- develop relationships with other organisations that share common cause with your own in order to be more effective in reaching potential volunteers;
- decide whether it would be more appropriate for your organisation to recruit volunteers in 'batches' or to engage with them on an individual basis, as and when they offer their services;
- think about whether or not you need a fixed time commitment from volunteers and if so, what it is;
- decide whether you need to be selective about volunteers or whether you would welcome all comers;
- decide, on the basis of the above, on an appropriate way for potential volunteers to find out about your organisation, and for you to find out about them. This may include more than one different kind of opportunity;
- if there are things that volunteers must know and/or be able to do before they start work with you, find ways of conveying this that will be accessible, interesting, enjoyable and non-threatening;
- decide how you and the volunteer will arrive at a shared understanding of what role the volunteer will carry out;
- decide how you will convey your organisation's values and code of conduct;

- work out how you and your colleagues can give the appropriate levels of personal and professional support to volunteers. Make sure that this a recognised responsibility of key people;
- ensure that on-going training and development is available to volunteers;
- find ways, if necessary in collaboration with other voluntary and community sector organisations and with community, further and higher education, to develop a career progression route for volunteers;
- find imaginative ways of providing practical support for volunteers, to remove or overcome the barriers that make it difficult for them to participate;
- make support for volunteers an explicit part of your organisation's budget, and search out funding that will help you develop this aspect of your work;
- think of ways of evaluating how effective your organisation is engaging with and developing volunteers. Hire external help to do this, if necessary;
- keep track of what volunteers do. Think of ways of assessing what impact their work has on the lives of the people they work with;
- document all of the above in any management or self-assessment report;
- find ways of rewarding volunteers for their efforts and celebrating their achievements.

Issues, challenges and trouble-shooting

- Ensure that volunteers can move on to other things once they have found their feet and grown in confidence and skill. At its best, working with volunteers enables them to realise potential they didn't know they had, so encourage people to fly the nest rather than limiting their horizions.
- Dare to define and use performance indicators that fit your own organisation. A culture of conformism and a fear of failure in the eyes of an external inspectorate or funding agency can lead organisations to fall into a frenzy of paperwork. Don't. All organisations in receipt of public funding are expected to demonstrate that they are making a difference. It's no longer possible to say, 'My funder doesn't understand me'. But find relevant and useful ways of measuring and judging your own performance – and improving it. That's what management's about!
- Keep abreast of all the government policy initiatives that relate to the voluntary and community sector. A regular trawl of key governments websites is a good idea. Include the Active Community Unit, the Neighbourhood Renewal Unit, RenewalNet,the Department for Education and Skills and the Learning and Skills Council.
- Manage paid staff seconded to voluntary organisations to support the management committee. This is a dilemma that often besets local authorities. Tension may develop between council officers and the management committee about just exactly who the member of staff reports to and what they should be doing.

Council officers need to make sure that lines of accountability are set out early on in this sort of arrangement and that they are reinforced, not just in writing, but through the regular professional supervision of the worker.

'*Pushing the Possibilities*' *programme*

Photograph courtesy of Way Out In Gateshead

Glossary

Active Communities Unit – a unit within the Active Communities Directorate of the Home Office committed to expanding and strengthening the capacity of the voluntary sector.

Civil Renewal Unit – a unit within the Home Office committed to community development (see below) and to encouraging people to take a role in the democratic process as it affects their communities.

Community capacity building – the process of helping people to develop knowledge and skills that will be assets to themselves, their family and their community.

Community development – an approach to transforming communities for the better based on building programmes of learning and action on a realistic assessment of residents' concerns, interests and aspirations.

Community intervention – strategies for getting to know what's **really** on residents' minds as opposed to what seems to be the case superficially.

Councils for Voluntary Service – voluntary organisations that support other voluntary organisations by, for example, providing training in relevant skills, helping with the preparation of funding applications and making representations on their behalf to other agencies.

Neighbourhood renewal – the rebuilding of communities by investing in people and what they have to offer, not just in the physical environment.

Para-professional – someone with a level of professional knowledge and skill that enables them to provide some immediate and valuable help to other people, but which does not equip them to take responsibility for others' development in the longer-term.

Performance indicator – a key feature of the job an organisation carries out. How well an organisation is performing can be judged by developing success criteria for each performance indicator and seeing whether or not the organisation achieves them.

Social infrastructure – the networks and human relationships that hold society together and help it run smoothly.

Sustainable development – in this context, the outcome of working with communities so that they develop the knowledge and skills to be able to solve their own problems and manage their own affairs.

Voluntarism – a system based on voluntary participation in a course of action.

Contributing organisations

Art and Soul Traders
The Lodge Arts Centre, Victoria Park, Anglesea Road, Portsmouth, Hants. PO1 3HJ.
Tel: 023 9287 0880. Emma Wright, Project Co-ordinator.
www.artful-lodgers.org

Community Learning Gateshead
Gateshead Council, Dryden Professional Development Centre, Evistones Road, Low
Fell, Gateshead, Tyne and Wear NE9 5UR.
Tel: 0191 4338646/8652. Kevin Pearson, Adult Learning Manager.

Women in Action Project
Horizon Housing Group Ltd.
2nd Floor Eastbourne House, 22-24 Gildredge Road, Eastbourne, Sussex BN21 4SA.
Tel: 01323 412535. Julie Gratton, Project Co-ordinator.

Promoting Adult Learning in the Community Project (PALS)
Learning Links (Southern) Ltd.
First Floor, 2A The Hard, Portsmouth PO1 3PU.
Tel: 023 9229 6460. Janet de Bathe, Chief Executive
www.learninglinks.co.uk

Manchester Women's Electronic Village Hall
Ada House, 77 Thompson Street, Manchester M4 5FY.
Tel: 0161 833 8800.
www.wevh.org.uk

MIND, Southampton and New Forest
Marcella House, Jones Lane, Hythe, Southampton SP45 6AT
Tel: 02380 841341. Diane Kitson, Project Manager.

Northern College for Residential Adult Education
Wentworth Castle, Stainborough, Barnsley, South Yorkshire S75 3ET.
Tel: 01226 776000. John Chapman, Course Leader.

www.northern.ac.uk
Norfolk Adult Education Service, Living Memory Project
Wensum Lodge, 169 King Street, Norwich.
Tel: 01603 674312. Margaret Plummer, Project Manager.

Riverside Credit Union
17 Central Parade, Speke, Liverpool L24 2SQ.
Tel: 0151 448 0565. Colin Farrell and Colin Strickland, Managers.

Time Together project, TimeBank
The Mezzanine, Elizabeth House, 39 York Road, London SE1 7NQ.
Tel: 0845 601 4008. Sarah Arnold, Manager.
www.timebank.org.uk

Useful contacts

Charities Evaluation Services – provides training and consultancy to the voluntary sector on quality and evaluation systems. www.ces-vol.org.uk

City of Guilds of London Institute – awarding body with course available for volunteers www.city-and-guilds.co.uk

Community Development Foundation – provides a wealth of guidance on developing good practice in community development. Training, publications and development support available. 60 Highbury Grove, London N5 2AG. Tel: 020 7226 5375. www.cdf.org.uk

Community Matters – the nationwide federation for community associations and similar organisations. Services include providing training in areas such as community capacity building, governance issues, community profiling and feasibility studies. www.communitymatters.org.uk

Community Service Volunteers – a UK-wide organisation providing brokerage service for volunteers and voluntary organisations needing each other's services, and media training for voluntary organisations. www.csv.org.uk

Development Trusts Association (DTA) – provides advice, support and training for community-led organisations wishing to develop and manage their own asset base. DTA, 1st floor, 9 Red Lion Court, London EC4A 3EF. Tel: 0845 458 8336. www.dta.org.uk

Institute of Volunteering Research – provides information about a variety of aspects of volunteering in the UK. 8 All Saints Street, London N1 9RL. www.ivr.org.uk

Learning Links (Southern) Ltd. – sells supporting materials to those who wish to develop PALS projects of their own. First Floor, 2A The Hard, Portsmouth, PO1 3PU. Tel: 023 9229 6460. www.learninglinks.co.uk

National Open College Network (NOCN) – awarding body with course available for volunteers. www.nocn.org.uk

National Council for Voluntary Organisations (NCVO) – the umbrella body for the voluntary sector in England. Represents the views of the voluntary sector to policy makers. Services include helpdesk, policy briefings, access to information networks and a wide range of publications. NCVO, Regent's Wharf, 8 All Saints Street, London N1 9RL. Tel: 020 7713 6161. www.ncvo-vol.org.uk

National Institute of Adult Continuing Education (NIACE) – offers many training events and publications related to community-based adult learning. NIACE, Renaissance House, 20 Princess Road West, Leicester, LE1 6TP. Tel: 0116 204 4200/4201. www.niace.org.uk

Northern Ireland Council for Voluntary Action (NICVA) – umbrella body for voluntary, community and charitable groups in Northern Ireland. NICVA, 61 Duncairn Gardens, Belfast BT15 2GB. Tel: 028 9087 777. www.nicva.org

Renewal.Net – a government website which is the 'online guide to what works in neighbourhood renewal'. www.renewal.net

Scottish Council of Voluntary Organisations (SCVO) – the umbrella body for voluntary organisations in Scotland. SCVO, The Mansfield, Traquair Centre, 15 Mansfield Place, Edinburgh EH3 6BB. Tel: 0131 556 3882. Also offices in Glasgow and Aberdeen. www.scvo.org.uk

The Joseph Rowntree Foundation – research and development organisation committed to social justice. Online book shop available. Recent addition: Active Ageing in Active Communities: Volunteering and the Transition to Retirement by Justin Davis Smith and Pat Gray. www.jrf.org.uk

The Scottish Community Development Centre – national organisation providing a wealth of guidance on developing good practice in community development. Training, publications and development support available. www.scdc.org.uk

Volunteering England – England's volunteer development agency 'works to promote volunteering as a powerful force for change, both for those who volunteer and for the wider community'. Website provides a range of resources mainly for managers of volunteers, and information about accredited training for managers of volunteers. www.volunteering.org.uk

Wales Council for Voluntary Action (WCVA) – the umbrella body for the voluntary sector in Wales. www.wcva.org.uk

References

1. *Social Justice: Strategies for National Renewal* (1994), Commission on Social Justice.
2. *Firm Foundations: The Government's Framework for Community Capacity Building* (2004) Civil Renewal Unit
3. *21st Century Skills: Realising our potential* (2003), Department for Education and Skills.
4. *Working Together: A strategy for the voluntary and community sector and the Learning and Skills Council*, (2004), Learning and Skills Council.